MW00943629

COME CLOSER

COME CLOSER

An Invitation

MILDA VAIVADA

Copyright © 2017 by Milda Vaivada
All rights reserved.

First Edition: September 2017

Edited by Raven Dodd, Preserving the Author's Voice
www.ravendodd.com

ISBN-13: 978-1976491092
ISBN-10: 1976491096

Library of Congress Control Number: 2017915500
CreateSpace Independent Publishing Platform
North Charleston, SC

DEDICATION

For the singing trees of Elm Street and to the creative force of nature that sustains the universe. For my precious family: my daughter Daiva, my son Colter and his wife Debbie, and my sweet granddaughter Vienna who inspire me to protect their natural inheritance and to all children everywhere who will inherit this earth.

"Trees are the earth's endless effort to speak to the listening heaven." Rabindranath Tagore

INTRODUCTION

July 31, 2017

I am not someone who cries easily or even one to really show emotion. It was the training from childhood, having a father who worked as an agent for the CIA. A poker face, when asked probing questions, was mandatory. One developed the art of never being too vulnerable. I was instilled with the responsibility that the survival of our family, our country, and indeed the world depended upon this skill. But that is a story for another time.

In July of 2017, everything shifted. That innate reserve fell away. My daughter Daiva and I had come to Lithuania for a heritage tour. Being 100% Lithuanian (my daughter 50%), we wanted to find our roots, our ancestors, and our connection to the homeland—the country from which my grandparents had emigrated to America in the early 1900s. The moment we stepped off the plane onto the tarmac in Kaunas, Lithuania, the world tilted and swirled. I was coming home, yet a home to which I had never been.

Everything was quivering with energy. The land seemed familiar and comfortable, but that was not rational, nor were the tears filling my eyes and sliding down my cheeks.

The airport was out in the country and surrounded by a thick, immense forest. I felt the trees moving and bending to catch a glimpse of us as we descended the stairs of the plane. They were waving a greeting, as if we both had been waiting, longing for this moment for lifetimes.

Over the next few weeks of our journey, all was illuminated. Hidden gifts and discoveries of pure gold were revealed, like the Temple of Milda, the Lithuanian pagan Goddess of Love. A fire on her altar is kept burning. We were completely immersed in nature and sacred groves. Since childhood, these landscapes had been calling to me in a distant misty dream, trying to make themselves known.

I did not hear voices, but rather a song humming without words. It was a melody that would gently pass through, like the fragrance of jasmine, and leave a lingering yearning. I heard a beckoning that would make me pause from whatever busyness occupied me. Something from which I had been separated was calling and now celebrating my return. Finally, I understood the experiences and communication with the nature realms I had growing up.

As you read the stories in this book, and consider your own relationship with the nature realms, know that this story is about you. This invitation to COME CLOSER is for you. This is your journey and legacy to discover.

Milda Vaivada
Naples, Florida

"In wildness lies the hope of the world." John Muir

1

RUN AWAY

Dearest beloved, the pleasure of your company is requested. You are on the guest list if this book has come in to your life. You are invited to come closer, lift the veil, and open the garden gate into the spirit world of nature. Enter the realm of trees, plants, fairies and devas, beings seen and unseen, known and unknown.

The earth is hosting your home-coming celebration. The festivities are in your honor. You have been missed, and all relatives of this world, sentient and non-sentient, want you to be reunited with them after a long and lonely separation. - Milda's Muse

1954

I had to run away. Finally, I knew exactly what I needed to do . . . run away from home, from this house. That was it. Head out and start walking down the road and keep on walking. It would be at dusk, so I could still see but be less visible. No one would notice until I didn't show up at the dinner table in the evening. I would bundle some clothes in a small piece of fabric and tie it to a long stick, like the hobos do in the cartoons, and carry it over my shoulder. It felt so liberating to have a plan . . . free to walk into my destiny. I would not suffocate, staying in a life where I did not fit or have a future. That afternoon I had left playing with the kids down the street and burst into the house to ask my mother a burning question.

"When I grow up, do I have to get married?"

Startled by my question, my mother, who rarely looked at me directly, turned to look at me in the eyes while drying her hands with a dishtowel.

"Why no, sweetheart. You certainly don't have to get married, but you are only five years old, so you have a long way to go before then. Why are you asking?"

"I am so glad," I said, extremely relieved, "because there is not one boy in this neighborhood I would want to marry." Roy Rogers was the one who had already captured my heart, but this question had been a huge weight on me. I had other deep concerns about what one had to do in adulthood, but at least now I knew I didn't have to get married. The world and my future opened up with this worry lifted.

Then there was the incredible dream I had the night before. So strange—so real, so vivid. In the dream it was a sunny afternoon. Since I was not old enough for school, my mother took me with her when she went to the store. She left me outside the front of the store while she went inside to shop. On the sidewalk, there were different stationary kid's rides like the ones in a carnival. I climbed in the small one that was an airplane, and even though I didn't have a quarter to put in the slot, it started moving up, down, and around on its own.

The plane suddenly came alive. It lifted off the ground with me in it and shot like a rocket up into the sky, going deep into outer space and the dark as night sky. The earth became as small as a marble and then disappeared from my view altogether. I held on as the tiny plane kept traveling upward straight into the blackness. Even as the plane and I hurled through space, everything was mysteriously, softly still and silent. It felt like the sensation of being underwater. There were stars as small as glitter scattered in the distance.

I was amazed and not at all afraid. I felt totally safe. The entire universe surrounded me, and it was extraordinary—just me in this vast galaxy and the overwhelming sense and presence of love. I became aware that I was not alone but enveloped by a hum emanating from the emptiness. Everything was so familiar and comfortable . . . like arriving at my real home, where I belonged and was protected.

For a while we just floated—drifting quietly with no sense of time. Suddenly the plane came back to life and started to descend to earth, landing in a vast field. It did not crash but came to a gentle swooshing stop as if it were a bird landing on a calm lake. During the flight day had turned into night, so I couldn't make out anything except the child's airplane in which I was sitting. It was eerie and moonless as I observed the landscape. There didn't seem to be anything around. The treeless field was not familiar.

Off in the distance, a small white boxy house appeared. I started walking toward it. Only the inside lights of the house were on, shining through the window. It looked as if it were a stranded spaceship that had just fallen to earth. As I walked closer, I felt life inside the house. Reaching the door, I paused and asked myself, "Do I really want to go in?" Even though I had not knocked, the door opened and a bright light cascaded over me as I stood on the small stoop. The glare blinded me, so I couldn't make out the face of the person standing in the doorway. This person didn't speak but mentally pulled me in, as if expecting and awaiting my arrival. Hesitating, I stepped inside the house—then with a jolt and a gasp I instantly woke up, disoriented.

Opening my eyes and looking up at the mattress springs above me, I realized I was back in my bunk bed. The house was silent as if covered in a blanket. My brother Tony in the bunk above me, my sister Vivian in her crib by the window, and my parents in their room were all sleeping. I knew who they were, but I wasn't sure who I was anymore. Wide awake, I suddenly felt like a stranger in a strange land.

In the morning the dream was still with me. It had felt so real. I wondered if it had been real. At breakfast Tony lined up Cheerios and Kix in front of him to create a wall of cereal boxes so we didn't have to see each other across the kitchen table. I was sitting there as usual but not a part of what was going on. My awareness now was that of an observer. Everything had shifted. I wasn't sure if maybe I was in another dream. How did one know what was real? What did being alive mean in the first place? What was life? After my experience of being in outer space, this was now my most important question. What was life? Before leading a grown-up life, wasn't it normal and necessary to have an answer to this question? Didn't everyone want to know the meaning of it all . . . the reason for being?

From my experience, looking to the adults around me for answers was a dead end. As far as I could tell, no adults asked any important questions. Their world was filled with mundane concerns, which made little sense to me. They were preoccupied and oblivious. I wanted to make them stop and look around. I realized I would have to find the answers to my questions on my own, and I didn't want to wait until I was in first grade and could learn to read.

I started getting ready to escape. Since my mother usually made our peanut butter and jelly sandwiches, I tried to remember how she did it. I should have learned earlier. A few pieces of plain Monk's bread would have to do. Clothes, toothbrush, pajamas . . . I couldn't find any fabric to carry them in. Running away was more complicated than I anticipated. Better to just bolt. When the time came, I raced out the front door. It was cloudy, so the sunset was early and the sky grey.

Since I had no idea where I was going to go, instinct made me turn right, away from town. Walking quickly, I was safely out of view of the house and steps closer to my new life. I had not gotten to Chain Bridge road, when my father pulled up beside me in our black Packard.

"Where do you think you're going?"

My brilliant future collapsed as he leaned over to open the heavy car door for me to get in. My father did not mention or discuss the episode after we pulled into the driveway. Having failed at my escape, I was escorted back into the house. Nothing had changed; there was no interruption of the normal routine that night.

If I couldn't run away, at least I could go outside and be alone. We lived in McLean, VA, which then was a rural area close to Washington, DC. The woods were just beyond our back yard. That was my retreat. I went out to the woods directly after returning in the front door. Sitting under my favorite maple tree amidst the wild fragrance of honeysuckle, I could be in peace with my question. It felt that trees held the answer to the mystery of life and would reveal it to me if I could be still enough to listen for the answer. If I were quiet enough, I could sense it on my skin, feel it inside myself, see it through my closed eyes, and smell it in the moist mossy air.

I made myself a nest in the damp leaves. Immersing myself with the tree, everything came alive and began humming. It was the same hum I had heard in outer space during my dream. Every mulberry leaf, blade of grass, twig, vine, rock, butterfly, bumblebee and bird were making the same sound and singing the same song. Everything in the wild places of our yard had a perfection and a completeness. Every creation was enough—every creature was exactly what it was meant to be. The maple tree fulfilled its purpose by simply being a maple tree. It held both the question and the answer to the meaning of life.

I tried to blend into the tree and be at one with its completeness. To just be. To catch a glimpse of the rapturous knowing from the trees that the reason for existence, for my existence, was existence itself. What is life? Life itself, fully experienced, is the meaning. Life doesn't require explanation, definition, or analysis. Being alive is the purpose of life. Euphoric with this stroke of insight, I raced from the woods across the yard in the twilight and up the back steps to the screen door leading into the large back porch.

I hesitated to go into the house and have my magic spell broken. The wooden, screened porch door creaked as I opened it—a comforting sound. I crossed the porch. The kitchen light was on inside the house, and I could see my mother's back as she stood at the stove. I thought to myself, *I don't know who she is, not really.*

As I walked into the hot stuffy kitchen heavy with cooking smells, my mother, not turning around but continuing to stir her pot, said to me, "I hope you didn't get poison ivy all over you, being in the woods. Go tell Tony dinner is almost ready."

Passing through the kitchen into the dim living room, I crossed quickly in front of my father who was staring at the TV. He was sitting in his large red chair that took up most of the living room, with his evening Manhattan balanced on the wide armrest. He was focused on the CBS evening news with Eric Sevareid. I admired Eric Sevareid and thought he was an adult who would ask important questions. As I crossed in front of my father to find my brother, he made not the slightest acknowledgement of my presence as if I were invisible, a ghost. Or maybe he was the ghost.

At that moment, I decided to keep my precious discovery about nature and the meaning of life to myself. No one would care or understand. It was my delicious secret.

"To live is so startling it leaves little time for anything else." Emily Dickenson

2

WILD CHILD

It is hard for the mind to see beyond what it already knows, but one's imagination—felt and even experienced through the heart—can visualize realities unimaginable to the mind. Because we exist through a vibration of love, whenever you are in a state of unconditional love, we can join with you and you with us. There is a simultaneous connection.

The connection is broken when the mind feels separation, causing upset and negative emotions that mask our primal connection. Being in nature, being in the wilderness, being in a garden, will naturally heal this misconception of separation. - Milda's Muse

1955

"Wild child," my mother used to say to me. "I never know where and what you are up to. I can't wait for you to start going to school." I didn't feel like a wild child, but I did always want to roam in the wild places. I was surrounded by wild places in northern Virginia, tucked between the farm pastures and the cluster of houses where we lived. Days were spent wandering and exploring. Fences between neighbors were rare, so wandering was natural.

A favorite expedition was to ride with my brother on his bike over the fields, far beyond our back yard to where the cow pasture was overgrown with tall grasses and wild flowers. With one swoosh of our large gauzy white butterfly catchers, we could scoop up dozens of brilliant butterflies. There were hundreds of them, all in different colors, sizes, and patterns. We peeked at them up close and then let them go. The air was a soup of butterflies, dragonflies, grasshoppers, honeybees, bumblebees, gnats, moths, and thick swarms of tiny things with wings that swirled around us. There was so much life! Humming, buzzing, fluttering and jumping filled this wild world.

Walking among the tall stalks of grass, top heavy with seeds that brushed our chins, our clothes were covered in sticky green hitchhikers. Winged tufts went airborne from the dandelions and milkweed. The old wooden gate was barely visible, covered in honeysuckle vine that climbed and tumbled over it. We made a snack from picking off the yellow and white blossoms and licking the clear sweet nectar drops on the ends of the delicate inside stems. The wild places spoke to us with a full symphony of voices both in movement and stillness. Our escapades followed the unpaved one lane cuts in the brambles and woods that most often narrowed to pathways where we had to leave our bikes and go farther on foot. The woods held mysteries like the old civil war jail house, hidden streams and secret hiding places. Every day was a day of discovery.

When I finally started first grade, my walk to school was straight down Elm Street, the narrow paved road in front of our house. Elm Street stretched straight into the center of McLean and was lined the entire way on both sides by enormous graceful elm trees. Their branches, rising from tall black tapered trunks, reached over the road touching at the top in a leafy green canopy. Walking through the long cool shady tunnel they created felt like walking through the center of the world. I heard them singing, not so much to me but to each other. They were the singing trees. They knew everything, holding the earth and the sky together with me in it.

"I would feel more optimistic about a bright future for man if he spent less time proving that he can outwit Nature and more time tasting her sweetness and respecting her seniority." E.B. White

3

ELM STREET

When you touch a tree, you are communicating with all trees. Your energy goes into the tree you are touching, down to the roots and through a network of roots that acts like an electrical grid sending a signal to all the other trees on earth. They are all connected. The forests and all the creatures within them say, "Embrace us. Be full with us, and don't pull away. Rather, do come closer. We are one and the same. Yes, please come closer. We are inviting you in!

When a tree is cut down without acknowledgment or apology, the trauma the tree experiences is felt globally within the plant kingdom. Conversely, when a tree is touched with tenderness, the love energy exchanged has a global healing effect. It helps keep the world from unraveling. - Milda's Muse

1956

After the summer of 1956 when I turned seven, my father was assigned overseas so our family relocated to Buenos Aires, Argentina. Once we settled into our new home in Martinez, a residential area just outside Buenos Aires, the adventures began. The first month our car was stolen, and since my parents were told that it most likely was stolen by the police, they never replaced it as it would just be stolen again. From then on for almost three years, except when we took a taxi in Buenos Aires, I did not see the inside of a car. All getting around was by foot or bicycle and transportation by train, *colectivo*, or school bus.

It was a perfect place for a wild child. My playmates and I roamed and explored freely. Everything was within reach. At the international school Escuela Lincoln where we were enrolled, my circle of friends spanned the globe: Thai, Japanese, Italian, Danish, British, and of course Argentinian. My father complained the Argentine government was a mess, but to me life in this amazing country was glorious, free, and a never-ending adventure. Every new friend, every unexplored corner and fresh vista, promised a world of discovery.

The houses in Martinez were close together but separated by high privacy walls, perfect for scaling and investigating what secret places were hiding on the other side. Brilliant white sidewalks lined with "soldier like" Seville orange trees connected every house's front door. Our live-in maid Juanita made us marmalade from the tart oranges that covered the trees. The neighborhood streets were narrow and full of kids. Few cars ever disrupted our games of kick ball or tag.

The identical German twin sisters who lived in the house directly across from ours dominated our block, cruising up and down the street on their impressive chrome and white scooters with giant fat tires. I wanted to meet all my potential new playmates in the neighborhood. As soon as my tricycle was unpacked from its long journey, I headed out to ride down the sidewalk. The twins' shiny scooters seemed so superior to my pink tricycle with its plastic streamers coming from the ends of each handlebar.

As I turned the first corner, my excitement and anticipation turned immediately to horror and embarrassment when I spotted two older boys on their two-wheel bicycles headed toward me. I felt so humiliated and childish riding my Tinkerbell tricycle.

They looked so high and commanding on their bicycles, barely having to hold on to the handlebars. Desperate that they might get a glimpse of the little *gringa* looking ridiculous riding a tricycle, I turned in an instant and peddled as fast as I could directly back into our garage.

Panting, I sat on my tricycle in the dark without moving to make sure the coast was clear before coming out. I never rode my kiddie tricycle again and did not re-appear on the street where the boys lived until I had struggled through learning to ride a two-wheeler. The day I first rode my bicycle, tall and proud and making my grand entrance passing the boys, I felt like Dale Evans riding on Buttermilk. Empowered from then on and quickly bored with the local boys, I ruled the world and pushed its boundaries, which consisted of how far I could ride and not get lost.

Allowance day was always eagerly awaited as it meant a bike trip to the local stationary store. Although tiny, the *tienda* was filled from top to bottom like one of the miniature ships inside the bottle, with every pencil, pencil box, pencil sharpener, eraser, pen, notebook, paper doll, game, puzzle, zippered bag, school supply, scissor, colored paper, and art supply ever imagined or invented. The strong, intoxicating cowhide smell, mixed with the scent of glue and ink, came from the leather satchels, book bags, brief cases and back packs jammed together and hanging low from the ceiling like bats in a cave.

The treat I waited for all week was when the shopkeeper brought out the large thick and cumbersome album of the most special creation ever produced by grown-ups—*figuritas*. My eyes laughed and danced as the pages of brightly illustrated cut out images of fanciful flowers, birds, butterflies and kittens were turned, and the glitter which covered the *figuritas* was all over my hands and clothes. Each week one new special *figurita* was added to my treasured collection.

I was heartbroken when my father's tour came to an end, and I had to say goodbye to my life and all my friends in Martinez to return to the US. What had been a foreign country when we arrived in Argentina had become home. Arriving back in the US and McLean, what had been home had changed and was now a foreign country to me. Destruction was all I could see where our neighborhood had been. It had been trampled to the point of being unrecognizable. Elm Street had been widened and the elm trees sacrificed for the expansion. They were completely gone, the majestic embracing elms that had held life together— gone. I had not been there to protect them as they had watched over me.

I kept asking my parents, "What grown-up would do this? Who would let this happen? Why did it happen?" It was incomprehensible to me.

"Development," my mother would say, as she changed the subject to look at her "To Do" list of errands and sort through her grocery coupons. The shock of it went deep, and I felt totally wounded, empathetically experiencing the pain, bewilderment, and betrayal the elms must have felt as the chain saw felled them down. With the elm trees gone, I felt a piece of my soul had died with them. Did the elms even have a voice as to their destiny? Was that voice heard?

The four-lane road that used to be Elm Street was now clogged with cars. The entire area had been zoned commercial. Low office buildings and parking lots were being built where the neighborhood kids used to play. The houses still standing where our neighbors used to live had commercial signs in front. The house across the street was now "McLean Insurance Co."

Our house too was about to be torn down. My parents had sold it to a developer who bought it for the land. I had no power to save it. Everything that had been around us was disappearing and soon gone: the elms, the expansive yards, the neighbors, the fields, the chickens, my favorite tree, the woods and the blackberries. Lady, the pinto horse, eating the grass in the meadow by our house, who loved the corn cobs we brought her as a treat, the butterflies we chased— all of it gone—dug up, thrown in a heap and burned into a pile of ashes. What had been my world was carved, graded and then paved over. A nameless, faceless destructive force had invaded and seized every living thing defenseless against it, including me.

The force had moved beyond our street and overtaken our favorite spot for winter sledding, a small road that rose high and cascaded down one of the tallest hills around. When the first real Virginia snow turned the hill road into a sleeping white polar bear, kids came from everywhere, pulling their racers behind them to sled down its back. Adults with thermoses followed behind. The road would be closed to traffic to allow for full enjoyment by everyone where the sledding continued from dawn to dusk. Now it was gone. It was all gone.

The middle of the hill had been cut through and shaved down, so what had been the high crest of the road was now at the bottom of a wide canyon. This new valley had left the houses on either side of the old road teetering atop a cliff, carved from what had once been their sloping front yards. The Swindler's house, where we would go to get warm and dry out our wet socks and boots, could not be entered through the front door because the doorstep was too close to the edge of the cliff. It was too precarious.

Again, I asked myself, "Who would allow this violation of where we lived?" This violation of the landscape. As part of the landscape, I was being attacked with it. It was personal, making me ill. Everything that had been wet and squishy in the spring, gentle and green in the summer, crispy brown in the fall, and white and soft in the winter, was now covered in a hard crust of cement. All the creatures that had been humming, buzzing and whispering were silent and missing. What was left was harsh and noisy. Every rolling hill we had roamed, wild wood where we had played and every secret hiding spot had been flattened and hardened.

The gentle inviting, embracing landscape of my childhood had been tortured, paved, and painted with stripes. My heart was in pain. Cars were welcome, and kids were not. As children, we had walked or ridden bikes everywhere. Cars were now king, and it was too dangerous for us to walk on or cross the new wide roads. Our world was restricted by the boundaries of highways. Movement was limited to only where an adult would drive you. My world shrank to the back seat of a car and freedom relinquished to the adult who was in the driver's seat.

Not being able to move back into our old house on Elm Street (as it had been sold for development), my parents bought one of the last remaining farm houses in the area. The two-acre property on Ingleside Avenue had a big red ramshackle barn, collapsing chicken coop, stone well house, and an old apple and pear orchard. Built on a high rise, our new "old" homestead was still surrounded by original beautiful maple trees, trees that were perfect for climbing. The trees seemed to welcome me and the ascent was easy. Once situated comfortably in the hollow created where two thick branches joined, I would spend hours high in the treetop analyzing the world beyond.

Most of the land that had belonged to the original farm had been sold off in small lots devoid of trees, to build ranch style houses. I had already promised myself never to get married but added mentally that I would never live in one of the stupid suburban houses that dotted our street. Instead, I would live in a tree house like the people did in *Swiss Family Robinson*. There was still a patch of woods beyond the guttered dirt road behind the barn. When not in one of our trees, I would wander in those woods. The trees were my best friends, and I thought perhaps they had also known the elms before they were cut down. Maybe, before the highway separated them, they had sung songs to each other through the breezes. But the

27

singing elms were gone, and traffic noise was all I could hear in the woods.

While we were out of the country, a new grammar school had been built, so my walk to school in the 4th grade was no longer down Elm Street. Now, I walked over the country road that followed the hills and fields of the large Carver Farm, the last working farm around McLean. The white wooden Carver farmhouse had a beautiful front porch, and from where it sat atop the highest hill, it seemed to smile down on us as we passed by on the road below. I was so glad I could still walk to school. The landscape had some semblance of what I remembered before leaving. The patches of woods gave me comfort. (The seasons and school years were reversed in South America, so even though I was just starting 4th grade, it was already spring in the American school year.)

Only a few weeks into the beginning of this new life, the walk to school turned into a walk across a battlefield. The Carver Farm was being developed into the Broyhill Estates, a new housing project. Huge yellow monster machines with giant tires that looked like reptiles, were racing across the road and the fields devouring everything. The green hills were being carved out by large scoops extending from the machines, their gouged-out bodies brown and exposed like the insides of a possum run over by a car.

Terrified that we might get trampled by the charging dinosaur machines, we scattered in different directions like scared cats and ran most of the mile to Churchill Elementary. The caterpillar machines were crisscrossing the farm, digging a spider web of new roads. A pack of wild mechanical beasts had descended, dismembered the hills, and then tossed their body parts into a freshly dug mass grave. Soon, I was sitting again in the back seat of a car being driven to school. It was too dangerous, the construction vehicles far too reckless for any child to walk safely to school.

The trees and the land had no voice, and as children neither did we. Together we were plowed under by "development," which showed no remorse. At nine and a half years old, I felt responsible for what had been done, although it was something over which I had no control. I needed to make an apology to nature on behalf of humans, but how? How would I ask forgiveness from nature after the adults had so damaged it? Was I considered one of "them," the humans? How would I cope having to grow up into the adult world that was destroying everything it touched? It felt unresolvable. There was no way to resist. The only option was to recoil from it, not participate in it, and go back to my home in the stars. Being born in this body was a mistake. I wanted to stop being a human and have the universe realize who I really was.

The universe needed to come for me and take me back. Perhaps I wouldn't be recognized unless I was in the woods. The forest became my sanctuary. Even in winter, I would go into snowy woods at night to be with the dark, misty silent trees. I would sit as still as the air and hope "they" would recognize me and take me home. I just wanted my body to vanish, to disappear and be a part of everything, to blend with the snow and the dark sky and the cold stillness of the woods. I wanted a life full of mystery and an existence apart from anything human.

As much as my being ached to blend into the woods, no matter how long I sat there, in the end I was still there as me—a human. Frigid and disappointed, I would go back to my room. The plants, pine trees, snow, logs, and the night sky all had a purpose to be what they were in their fullness, but humans seemed to have no purpose and were only an intrusion on the planet and natural world. How would I as a child of nine, about to grow up into this adult heartless world, cope?

COME CLOSER

"The temple bell stops but I still hear the sound coming out of the flowers." Matsuo Basho

4

WHAT IS GOD?

The force of love is what creates healing, and through love and gratitude we can communicate with you. Like radio waves we are always out there, but we need the correct frequency to come in and be heard. Love is the frequency, and once we resonate in love, we can hear each other loud and clear. You are always connected with us when you are in a state of love and gratitude.
- Milda's Muse

1958

Nature was its own reason for being . . . I had figured this out. It did not need a purpose. But what about humans? What was their purpose? I was utterly frustrated that I could not drop my human form, blend into the woods, and disappear back into the natural world where I belonged. Feeling stranded in an alien world of adults, I was perplexed as to whether any grownups had questions about being alive or even wondered about it.

My Grandmother Ba, born in Lithuania, was raised Catholic, but when she came to America by herself at 16, she was a declared atheist and had a pagan spirit. Ba spoke of the abuses by the local priests back in her village and how they terrorized the peasants. For instance, the priests would declare that on Sunday there was going to be a blessing of the goats. All the villagers had to bring their goats with money tied to their horns in order for the priest to bless the goats. No money—no blessing—and the goat was cursed. She was allergic to the Catholic Church and everything for which it stood.

Both my parents, also Lithuanian, were basically agnostics. Their only religious conviction was to the observation of politics, current affairs, and books. My father's book collection covered the breadth and width of our house and contained what I thought must be all the factual knowledge known to man. I was on my own trying to make sense of man's place in the natural world.

Although almost 10, I had never been to a church. There were lots of churches in McLean, and it seemed to me there might be something going on inside these churches that could be relevant to my quest. I wondered what wisdom might be discovered. Sunday mornings at our house were filled with the Sunday New York Times and news programs. A lot of information but not much wisdom from my point of view. Restless to go on a church field trip, I pestered and cajoled my parents to take me to a church, any church. They kept promising. One chilly but radiant early Sunday morning in March, while they were still sleeping, I woke them up by rudely shaking the covers over their lumpy, listless bodies. My father was snoring loudly. I didn't stop until one of them stirred and then turned over to acknowledge my irritating demands.

"Please take me to church," I insisted. "Take me to a church. You promised!"

My father eventually gave in, and soon we were sitting on a long wooden seat in a large white room with high ceilings crowded with devout Christians in the McLean Baptist Church. We arrived late, so the bench was full, and my father and I had to squeeze in between the others to make a place for us to sit. The service had already started. With so many grown-ups in suits and coats around me, I couldn't see over their heads. They were all looking forward in the same direction at someone talking in the front of the room, with attentive but blank stares on their faces. I couldn't understand what the person was saying, and his voice was dull. He went on and on and was the only one speaking. It was not at all a discussion. How was anyone to learn anything if there was no discussion and you couldn't ask any questions? I had so many questions.

Frustrated, I looked up past the adult faces into the blank ceiling. This was not what I expected. I wasn't going to find any wisdom here if this was what "church" is. The man stopped talking, and suddenly everyone reached over to take out a heavy, stiff book that was in the back of the seat in front of them, then opened it and started singing. My father did the same and joined them in the singing, staring into the book. I was horrified. Why was he singing with these people? The words made no sense, and I was sure he never had seen them before.

Hearing his voice singing strange sentences about the lord made me nauseous. My father was an intelligent man, a man who had deeply complicated thoughts and only spoke when he had something profound to express. What had happened to him? He was scaring me. Everything about the church made me uncomfortable. I just wanted to be outside in the fresh air and back in our yard to see if any spring flowers had started to bloom. It might be warm enough so that I could only wear a sweater, which would make it easier to climb trees.

Squirming, I asked my father, "Can we leave now?" I couldn't wait to be out of that place. Relieved, my father slid us out of the pew, and we made our escape, leaving everyone still singing.

"Back so soon?"

Mother was standing at the stove as we opened the side kitchen door and walked in. I could smell French toast and coffee and hear the voice of a male reporter on the Sunday morning news coming from the TV in the family room. My hope that some clue related to my question could be found in a church was deflated. I had gone to a church, and there was nothing for me there—not anything. *And*, I thought to myself, *the building itself was especially ugly.* As soon as breakfast was over, I climbed high into the upper branches of the maple tree.

My parents must have discussed the need for my brother, sister and I to have a more relevant place to satisfy our spiritual interests, for everyone's sake. The next Sunday, they scooped us all up and into our faded blue Valiant sedan for the trip to Oakton, VA. The two-lane Chain Bridge Road quickly brought us out of McLean into rolling farm country. Sitting in the back seat, the up and down, up and down hills felt like one long endless roller coaster. It was an exciting journey that would have been too dangerous on this road during the freezing winter. The chilly air left over from

February had mellowed into March drizzle, even though the fields we saw from the car window matched the brownish-gray of the sky.

Next winter, we should figure out how to sled on these hills when there is a snow day, I thought despite the unfamiliar remoteness of the area. After many miles of driving up, down, and around hills that sometimes grew into small mountains, I realized our car was the only one on the road. I was glad the old Valiant hadn't broken down because there would not have been anyone around to help us. We had not seen a single house, even in the distance. It was wonderful!

After what seemed like days, the road came to a cross road, and an old white building with a garage stood where the roads intersected. I could see a faded sign over the closed peeling garage doors, "Tyson's Corner." It was Sunday, so everything was closed. In the dreary rain, the place felt like the Twilight Zone, where after a nuclear war the world had come to an end, and only a few people were left to survive in an empty eerie silent landscape. It felt as if the five of us in our "klunker" of a car were the last people left on earth. Luckily a nuclear bomb had not gone off since we left our house in Mclean because as soon we were driving into Vienna, suburban houses and shopping centers suddenly replaced the landscape of fields and farmland. I still didn't see any people except the ones inside all the cars. They appeared as the road widened from two lanes to four then six lanes and as the cars were now stopping at a traffic light.

It was slow passing through Vienna, but we finally came to Oakton—a quiet green place with large old trees. We turned into the lot of a two-story, red brick building right on the main street and parked. Opening the car door, we immediately knew spring had arrived in Oakton. You could smell it in the rain. The Unitarian Church was inside a friendly-looking building that was an elementary school during the week. I liked it. We were late, and the Sunday school class had already started. Our family never got anywhere on time.

The Sunday school teacher was wearing a pretty shirt dress with a pattern of soft colored flowers. She was surprised when we walked in, interrupting the class, but then seemed glad to have new students and welcomed us. We felt awkward but happy to be there even though all the kids looked up from what they were drawing on colored sheets of construction paper, crayons in their fingers, to stare at the newcomers. Quickly bored with us, they went back to their project. The Sunday school teacher had smooth blond hair that curled under and was as cheerful as her dress.

Handing us our supplies, she said, "I want you to draw a picture of God." I must have appeared startled at such a direct assignment. "Just choose your favorite color paper and draw what you think God looks like," she said encouragingly. Then she left me to myself. I opened the brand-new box of 16 crayons and brought the waxy tips to my nose for a whiff. *The best smell in the world*, I thought to myself. *Nothing is as wonderful!* There was a ritual for opening a new box of crayons. My system was to leave all the crayons in the box and only pull out each color one at a time as they were used and carefully replace them before taking out another. I chose a dullish blue piece of paper but couldn't decide what crayon color to begin with.

Uninspired, I sat there. "I want to know what God is, not who he is," I said to myself. But no one seems to ask that question. *What is God?* I thought. I felt resigned because of course, to everyone but me, God was a who, not a what. To me, God was so much bigger than a who. Wanting to please the teacher, sitting alone at the too small classroom table, I picked a silver-gray crayon and drew an old man's face in the top right corner of the paper. He had long white hair and a long white beard. *That is what she thinks God should look like*, I assured myself. In the lower left corner, I added a circle, which I filled in with green and blue crayons, so the old man was looking down on Earth from the sky. The teacher came over to where I was working.

"What do you have to show me?" she said, smiling a genuinely interested smile. I handed her my drawing of the floating old man's face looking down on the also floating earth assured of her approval. I was very surprised to see a disappointed expression come over her face.

"Is this all you think God is? A man with a white beard?"

For a moment, I sat embarrassed and unresponsive to her question. "Of course, I don't think that is all that God is, but I thought that's what you thought God was," I said loudly to myself in my mind. Then speaking meekly, I confessed, "No, I really don't think that's what God is."

Then she said, "Well, why don't you think about it, and when you come next Sunday I want you to draw another picture of what God really is to you, OK?"

Dizzy from having an adult interested in my opinion about the nature of God, I was quiet in the car on the drive home, absorbed in my inquiry. The rain had turned into a thick fog, covering the landscape that had been so captivating earlier that morning. When we pulled into our gravel driveway, I was in another world. "1229 Ingleside Ave" was still on the mailbox, but everything seemed completely new as if I had never seen it before. My parents and brother and sister had gotten out of the car, but I was still sitting in the back seat repeating the question, "What is God? What is God?"

In a daze, I opened the car door and put my feet on the ground to stand up. The pebbles and gravel were so alive, almost dancing even though the rain had covered them in bits of dirt. Next to the driveway, the land rose to create a small mound that leveled out into our front yard where some daffodils were sending up green shoots, and some were blooming. It was still drizzling, but the daffodils seemed to be humming a yellow tune in the rain and were happy and sunny.

In a flash, everything was glowing and suddenly alive. The grass, the flowers, and the maple tree were pulsing with life, then dissolving as if in a watery reflection, then reappearing. They were showing me that everything in life is created out of love. Love was the creative energy of the world. The daffodils, the soggy grass, and the tree were all telling me that they were "how love shows itself." They were pure love.

God is Love and Love is God and Love is everywhere! The awareness that the essence of the universe and creation of life was the vibration of Love put everything in a new order for me. This experience of what life was about was pivotal. The purpose of life—of human life—was to acknowledge, appreciate, and fall into the grace of this Love and reflect it back to all things. It came to me that the purpose of human existence was to be joyful in the beauty of this Love creation/vibration. Embrace it, take it in, marvel at its beauty, and cherish it.

"To cherish what remains of Earth and to foster its renewal is our only legitimate hope of survival."
Wendell Barry

5

IT'S ALL ABOUT OIL

The calling now is to interrupt this cycle of abuse. Intervene and free the beings who may not even be aware they are enslaved and bring awareness to the exploitation that is taking place. Our culture has enslaved just about every living and non-living being/thing from plants, animals, to rocks, mountains, forests, seeds, all growing things, and resources above and below the ground. The extent of this control is unprecedented in earth's history as we know it, and it is not sustainable. The sun is still an entity that has not been manipulated or subjugated—giving of itself freely to all.

This world is a co-creation of all entities. The beings are asking us to come closer . . . to put a big toe into the vast extension of who we really are and look at life from a different angle—that the earth and all it provides is there and created for our support but not for our greed. The beings are closer to us when we are in a state of joy and experiencing pleasure in the deepest sense from feeling a connection (emitting oxytocin, the love hormone) and experiencing the world through the wholeness within. When we are feeling pleasure and internal joy, we are closer to ourselves and the other realms.

Your life can be restructured to include all the things that bring you satisfaction and pleasure as they will strengthen your vibration and your energy, bringing energy to the planet and increasing the life force. - Milda's Muse

1960

Having had the awakening experience of love being the life force that sets creation in motion, I sought to understand how this insight could resolve the question: What was driving the unraveling and destruction of the natural world around me? What was the dark force tearing down the trees, shaving the hills, dissecting the farms, plowing over the streams and then covering it all with pavement? My wild child world of wandering in the woods and meadows was over and had been buried under the black hardness of parking lots.

I was on fire with this question. What was happening? Why was it happening? How could it happen? Who, what was doing this? Frantic to understand and stop it, I searched and searched for clues. What had changed? Everything was different. Then the answer came—it struck me—it was chilling and clear. I saw it. It was the cars. The invasion of giant machines rolling down pavement was to make way for the cars. All the highways, sprawling shopping centers, and vast acres of parking lots were for the automobile. Cars feed on gasoline, and gasoline comes from oil. I had unraveled the mystery. Following the trail back to the source, I found where the monster was hiding and looked it in the eyes. That was it—it was oil. It was all about the oil.

At that moment, feeling drained and inadequate against this force of greed, I made a personal pledge. When I grew up, I would never own a car. Even though I was years away from taking Driver's Ed in school, when the time came, I would not get a driver's license. I vowed I would never drive. I would not, could not contribute to the madness. I would not succumb to the sickness brought by the oil contagion. Years later, when the time did come, I completed the required Driver's Ed course but kept my promise not to get a license or car. On the day when they got their licenses, my friends were elated to be driving. To them, being able to drive meant freedom. I saw the car as the loss of freedom.

Choice had been removed. All the places we could walk or bike to had been made inaccessible by highways impossible or too dangerous to cross. Society had been tricked. Now, the only way to get around was by car. I was resolute and determined. I couldn't stop it but would not feed this beast that had devoured the wildness and wilderness of my childhood. The places where once I had been free to wander, were now only accessible and viewed through the small window of the rolling prison of an automobile.

COME CLOSER

"That which is not good for the bee-hive cannot be good for the bees." Marcus Aurelius

6

THE QUESTION

We cannot be separated from you just as you cannot separate your heart from your body . . . but you can forget it is even there as it pumps your life-giving blood. You can take it for granted, not show it love and gratitude, even abuse it—but it is there regardless, dedicated to your wellbeing. That is how we are with you. The only requirement is for you to remember and acknowledge the relationship. Miracles flow from that. Don't forget to love your heart and all other parts of your miraculous body. You are inseparable from them and they from you. We the trees are inseparable from you and you from us. - Milda's Muse

1962

In the fall of 1962, I was in the 7th grade at James
Fennimore Cooper Middle School in McLean. With
the Kennedy administration, there came a fresh
excitement in the air and new approaches. The
teachers were inspired by Kennedy and eager to try
new things. There was a sense of history in the making.
As awkward adolescents, we were dealing with the
dreaded physical fitness testing that was now
mandatory to comply with Kennedy's new physical
fitness standards for America's youth population. At
13, I was 5'6" and fully developed. My arms lagged in
strength, and I struggled to manage one chin lift.
Mostly, we all failed the mandates and felt very
blubbery.

Despite this, the school year started off with the
promise of new educational activities and
opportunities. Instead of the traditional separate
history and English classes, our school was
implementing a new concept of "team teaching"
historical and literary trends to create an overall
picture of the world's evolution. The new joint classes
were taught under the term World Civilization (WC).
The teachers were inspired by the fact that Kennedy
had brought on a White House Philosopher to serve
in his administration.

The team faculty, in an inspired move, made arrangements for the students of WC to take a field trip into Washington DC to meet the new White House philosopher. In preparation for this unique opportunity to interact with a true philosopher (Socrates and Plato came to mind), we were assigned to prepare a question to present to him. I was thrilled and terrified at the prospect of embarrassing myself and jeopardizing the reputation of JFC and thus took the challenge with great gravity. I wanted to construct a question worthy of a philosopher's answer. A question, the answer to which might save the world.

Having just read *All Quiet in the Western Front* and still plagued by nightmares about concentration camps, I was obsessed with the horrors, suffering, and destruction caused by war. It wasn't just the human misery that weighed on me but the collateral harm caused to the living creatures and the assault on the natural surroundings. The earth was being badly hurt, trees, animals, insects, birds . . . all vulnerable and innocent. So, this was the question I crafted and carefully rehearsed:

When mankind goes to war, why does he not think about the harm that is being done to the world of nature and all it encompasses? Why does he allow this damage to happen and not take responsibility for his actions?

This was going to be the moment—the moment of speaking up in defense of nature. Here was the golden opportunity to present this obvious concern to someone whose job it was to consider such basic questions and have a dialogue. Perhaps we could re-direct the course of human behavior and history. The anticipation as we rode the school bus into the District was electric. Totally focused, I practiced my question, reciting it over and over again in my mind. My brain was rumbling like a volcano about to erupt and send molten lava down my face. My body, neck, and shoulders were so tight I could barely breathe. I thought I might faint.

We numbered about 100 and once at our destination, we were escorted into a small auditorium inside the magnificent Old Executive Office Building next to The White House. The setting was intimate. The faculty was giddy with anticipation and got us settled quickly. When everyone was seated and all was quiet, the professorial looking philosopher entered. Wearing a dark greyish suit, tie and sweater vest, he came on stage and sat in an ordinary office chair set in the middle, directly in front of us. The house lights dimmed, and a soft downlight shone upon him.

He introduced himself and opened the floor to questions. There was silence and some squirming in the audience. *Courage*, I thought to myself. I was going to need my bravest instincts. This was the moment to speak for all the creatures who had no voice. The question was now a fireball in my throat that I couldn't wait to spit out. Staring straight ahead, I took the ultimate leap and raised my arm to be recognized.

Through the sound of my heartbeat pulsing in my ears I heard suddenly, from out of nowhere, a thunderous voice that shouted, "Do you believe in Jesus?"

As if we had just been slapped in the face, we all turned to see who had hit us. Again, "Do you believe in Jesus?" the angry voice demanded.

Another shock wave passed through from the assault of these words. "Are you a Christian?" the voice accused. Then I saw her. It was Carolyn. She was the vial source of these outbursts. Her pudgy face flushed with outrage. Carolyn, who never spoke a word in class to anyone but sat planted at her desk with a permanent grimace on her face, had morphed into a screaming banshee before our eyes.

It was as if a bomb had gone off, and her toxic words spewed a grey ash over everyone, including the philosopher. He did not respond to her attack. The room was frozen. No one, not even the faculty, knew what to do or how to react. They were the adults and yet did nothing. We were all catatonic with disbelief, fearful of another outburst. The room was smothered into silent submission. Paralyzed, no one asked a single question. There was no discussion, no enlightened discourse, no stimulating conversation.

I felt totally conflicted and defeated and could not find my voice. I looked to one of the faculty for a cue to encourage me to speak up, but the teachers, completely caught off guard by the episode, were downcast—pale with extreme embarrassment, disappointment, and defeat. How could all their brilliant expectations have been ruined like this, was the look on their faces. Unable to shift or retrieve the situation, they ended the afternoon early amidst the gloom.

I desperately had wanted to ask my burning question. It needed to be asked. This had been the moment. Instead, on the bus ride back to the suburbs, in my grief I swallowed the question and felt it settle as a permanent knot in my chest. No one said a word on the entire journey home. Carolyn relapsed into her brooding stupor. The teachers were in silent mourning and never acknowledged, mentioned or commented on the episode. It all felt very weird and unresolved. I don't know if they ever recovered.

COME CLOSER

"Munificent nature follows the methods of the divine and true, and rounds all things to her perfect law. While nations are convulsed with blood and violence, how quietly the grass grows." E.H. Chapin

7

THE CUBAN
MISSILE CRISIS

C ome closer. It is an invitation to be
willing to open up to a reality that
co-exists and co-creates with our own.
Once we stop and take a moment to
appreciate the miracle and mystery of life
and the world around us, we have taken
the first step closer to these realms and
initiated a relationship that was once a
part of our lives—a part of our lives
before the mental chatter and cultural
clutter caused a disconnection between
ourselves and the world of wonder.

Our being encompasses all the
worlds. One need only to be still and
listen, to step inside oneself and be
present in the moment, to open to the
love vibration that is the vibration of

creation and unites all beings through time, space, and form. It is the ultimate connection between all things.

- Milda's Muse

1962

Everyone had their eyes fixed on the TV monitor perched above the door that was the entrance to our 6th grade classroom. We were silent, we were watching, we were scared. There had been a series of drills over the last weeks. How to shelter under our desks for cover, how to evacuate the school. I had been having nightmares about being separated from my parents if the nuclear war came while I was in school. I dreamt that during the day everything would go dark and our school would be evacuated on buses to a safe location. There were long lines of buses taking us to a bomb shelter somewhere unknown, and I would never see my parents again. If we emerged after the bomb, the earth would be nothing but a pile of ash.

Now the showdown was happening right in front of us. We were watching it unfold. My hands were sweating and clasped tight on the top of my desk. On the screen we could see the Russian submarine. It was very still in the water, like an alligator I had seen on our trip to Florida. Sinister and unpredictable. The TV camera was looking down on it from a helicopter. It had been headed to Cuba, but now an American destroyer was parked in the water directly in front of it.

The teachers were grim faced as we listened to the voice of Walter Cronkite from the speaker. He only spoke a few words at a time. Everything was suspended in time. There were long pauses between his sentences. No one knew what was going to happen. No one was breathing.

Then the teachers exhaled as if someone who had a knife at their throats put it down and surrendered. An imminent danger, a life and death moment had just been diffused, and we lived to see it. There was relief that this hour in the classroom at WW Longfellow Junior High School would not be our last. Nobody moved or spoke as we watched the Russian submarine very slowly turn around.

"Those who can make you believe absurdities can make you commit atrocities." Voltaire

8

THE GOLD BRACELET

Perhaps the first step is to "come closer" to those around us in our community. Get to know them as people and not just as the bank teller, the grocery cashier, the postman, the garbage collector, etc. If we can stop and appreciate them—even if it is just sending a silent blessing—this can be a huge step toward re-connecting to the truth that we are still just a tribe, living in community.

Even though we have lots of stuff and gadgets, and individual pieces of land, property, and houses, we all still live on the same land. We are intertwined despite spending much effort at keeping each other out and separated. We prize our distance from each other and our separation. It is natural and instinctive for our species to be drawn to those we recognize as "ourselves," but the extreme of that is not mixing at all with those who are not like us. We see this intolerance especially with culture, religion, ethnicity, age, and health.

It is not natural to exclude and disenfranchise those who are not part of our socio-economic circle or age group. Everyone has something to contribute to the community and the planet as a whole. If we can appreciate this truth and honor each other, there will be less isolation and loneliness in our lives. - Milda's Muse

1963

The gold link bracelet my mother often wore on social occasions emerged from a dark story that deeply contrasted to the happy moments I associated with it. As children, we were unaware of the secrets associated with my father's time in the military. That was until I accidentally uncovered a cardboard box, containing small unmarked dusty black boxes in the attic, while rummaging through cartons of Christmas decorations.

All we knew from family discussions, when my father was less guarded, was that during WWII, he was an army intelligence officer under General Patton, living in London. Proficient in English, German, Polish, Russian, and Lithuanian, my father's language skills made him an asset to the intelligence war against the Nazis, the planning of D-Day and the invasion at Normandy. As far as we knew the story ended there.

I disliked the dank, dark airless attic space. It had no solid floor, so one had to straddle the beams sticking up between the awful pink fiberglass insulation and try not to fall through the ceiling. Being the "artistic" one of the family, I had the task of decorating our large showpiece of a holiday tree. Determined to make sure I found all the favorite elaborate Christmas balls my parents had bought when I was a toddler, and we lived in Munich in the early 50's during the German occupation, I braved the dreaded attic for one last look.

I was excited at first upon discovering what I thought was an overlooked box of the treasured ornaments. The identical black containers stacked inside, made of coarse fabric, looked like they had not been disturbed for a very long time. Pulling out one of the boxes and removing the top, I peered down expectantly at the contents. Holding the box in one hand and the top in the other, I stared inside for a long while, trying to process what I was seeing. Elegant shiny ornaments are not what I found but rather two piles, side by side of black and white photographs.

In the photos were stacks of naked human bodies. The bodies were not like any I had ever seen. I looked more closely. They were corpses. I started to get nauseous. The dead were totally emaciated with limbs as skinny as sticks and piled up like kindling in long rows—row after long row of bodies, stacked 10 high, one row behind the other all in front of what looked like factory buildings. Photo after photo of hundreds upon hundreds of gaunt faces with open mouths gaping in agony attached to emaciated bodies—some put in piles—others left in large heaps. It was too horrible.

I closed the top firmly on the box and took out another. Opening it, I saw the same haunting images with different industrial buildings in the background. Feeling confused and terrified that evil itself would escape from these photos and what they had captured, I shut the box and pushed it away. Racing down the metal folding ladder that led to the floor below, I was frantic to find my parents to tell them what I had discovered.

My father was silent, turning his head to the side and looking at the floor while listening to me. I was not in trouble for finding the box of secrets, but he would not respond or talk about it. My mother, seeing that there was no way to avoid an explanation of what I had witnessed, started to fill in the details.

After the invasion on D-Day, my father and his group of intelligence officers were charged with the task of immediately following on the heels of the Allied forces as they moved into Europe and drove out the Nazis. As the liberation army approached, the German troops retreated in haste from their occupied territory, without time to dismantle their death camps, dispose of records, or clean up evidence. My father's assignment was to seize and secure the concentration camps and document what had occurred. He was among the first persons to see close up what atrocities the Nazi's had been conducting.

When his team arrived, there were people still alive that had been held inside the prison barracks. The team's priority was to secure food and medical help to try to save as many people as possible from dying. No one could believe the horror of what had gone on in camp after camp, after each was liberated. Because my father spoke so many languages, he was one of the ones to—as quickly and efficiently as possible—interview the survivors to help locate missing relatives, reunite families and assist with relocating them to their towns and villages.

The gold bracelet had been a gift sent to my father, years later, by one of the men held in the camp who had survived and been freed when his camp was liberated. His wife had been shipped to another camp, and my Father searched for her in each camp they entered. Finally, he was able to locate her and bring them back together. The bracelet was a token of their gratitude.

How could humans inflict such suffering on each other? The adult world scared me. Nothing, not even children and the natural world, were safe from abuse. I was in total conflict about how to grow up in what was supposed to be a civilized society and became obsessed with the Holocaust and concentration camps. My siblings and I never were allowed to see the images from the camps again, nor did we want to. The few photos I had viewed had already given me nightmares.

Every night, I would say a personal prayer asking the angels for protection. I prayed for every family member by name and the entire world, all the living creatures within it, and especially the forests. Every morning, no matter how much I disliked waking up early to go to school, another prayer of gratitude came to my lips that I was not waking up in a cold concentration camp but safe in my own bed. In school, we read the diary of Anne Frank, and I felt immensely guilty that I had not been there to save her or protect her in some way. She would have been one of my friends; we shared so many thoughts and feelings. If she—as sensitive and beautiful as she was—could be killed, we could all be in danger.

The woods were my sanctuary. Being in nature was the healer. That would have been one of the worst parts of being in a concentration camp—never being able to find retreat from human suffering in the embrace of trees, or flowers or anything beautiful and natural. Being in the forest was being surrounded by love. There was no room for hate or torture in the radiance of the sunlight filtering through the branches of the maple trees, even when they were bare in the winter. Nature held the cure to ensure there would never be another concentration camp.

"The best remedy for those who are afraid, lonely or unhappy is to go outside, somewhere where they can be quite alone with the heavens, nature and God. Because only then does one feel that all is as it should be and that God wishes to see people happy, amidst the simple beauty of nature. As long as this exists, and it certainly always will, I know that then there will always be comfort for every sorrow, whatever the circumstances may be. And I firmly believe that nature brings solace in all troubles."

Anne Frank, *The Diary of a Young Girl*

Here is an advance look at the chapter, Lightning Bug Summer, in the upcoming Book Two of the Come Closer series.

LIGHTNING BUG
SUMMER

You were sent this invitation before. It has been sent over space and time as a gentle invitation to wake you from your sleep and dreaming. We will meet you in the quiet space under the tree. We will meet you in the quiet space while you are gazing at the starlit sky. We will meet you in the quiet space where you are full of love and gratitude—every time you are full of love and gratitude for the simplest things. We will find you, we can see you, hear you, and feel you. You glow like a firefly. - Milda's Muse

1999

"Hurry, hurry!" I called out from the deck. "You're going to miss it!" The June sun was dimming behind the very tall oak trees that made up our back yard. The house was a contemporary split level, so the upper deck seemed to fly off the back of the house far above the ground, thrusting one into the very top of the fully leafed trees. I was arranging the scattered outdoor chairs theatre style to give us a front row view. I could see that the vintage turquoise blue and white metal springy chairs had not been cleaned yet after being stored through the winter. They had old leaves stuck to them and little puddles with tadpoles in the seats. They must have been left out since last September and never put away. That used to be my job in May; clean the mildew, leaves, and grit off all the lawn furniture. I had enjoyed doing it because it meant that picnics and back yard 4th of July fireworks were almost here and my most favorite thing of all—lightning bugs.

There was no response from inside the house, so I left my setting up tasks to go open the half glass, half wood side door to find and motivate my audience. Looking through the glass into the kitchen area and den, the house had gone dark even though it was still light outside except for the bluish light of the TV and a farmhouse style light over the kitchen table. The dining/kitchen/family table had become my father's desk since his stroke, which had put him in a wheelchair part of the time. Even though he could sit in a regular chair and still walk some, he parked his wheelchair at the head of the table as if it were his throne.

His "desk" was entirely covered with piles of newspapers, clippings, cannibalized magazines, mail opened and unopened, files, postage stamps sorted into different plastic boxes, boxes of Christmas cards, rubber bands, boxes of paper clips, pens that had printed on them, "Property of the US Government," and half used paper napkins that he hoarded. He was busy shuffling papers. He said he was "getting organized," but everyone else called it "gerbling" because nothing ever got sorted, just moved from one pile to another.

Even though semi-retired after 50+ years as an agent and research analyst for the CIA, my father was still compelled to read at least the New York Times, Wall Street Journal, Washington Post (The Evening Star was no longer), and the Christian Science Monitor everyday along with every International news magazine ever published. We grew up in fear that if his task of reading all these periodicals was not fully completed, the entire world would unravel on the spot. His piles of clippings were never to be disturbed, and the stacks of editorials—well, they were the Holy Grail. Information was a weapon. Current events were of critical importance. Current events were the only thing of importance. The gathering of information kept us safe. It was, of course, information that was secret and private. We were not to touch anything or ask any questions.

My Mother was sitting in the beige, corduroy covered recliner in the den reading the Providence Journal, McLean's local paper, under a wobbly gooseneck lamp. The TV was on with the evening news but no sound. Coming inside from the breezy outside, the house felt stuffy and lifeless with my parents plastered in place.

"Come on, it's almost starting," I said, prying them loose from their respective spots. "I know our world is unraveling and descending into chaos, but there are other worlds out there."

I maneuvered my father's wheelchair out the kitchen door onto the deck and moved him up to the railing. Mother came along using her cane and sat in a deck chair beside him.

"Just watch," I said, and we sat there together without speaking.

Then it began, just a quick flicker at first in the grass below. Then another—then single random sparkles rising from the ground and more flickers of light—maybe a dozen in view. The mass ascension of lightning bugs was beginning. They rose silently like little lighthouses adrift in the dark signaling to each other, a shower of earthbound twinkling stars released from gravity and falling up to the sky. Now hundreds and soon thousands—little alien light beings from another realm, miraculous and mysterious—appeared. Wave upon wave filled the steamy night air, the first to appear now reaching the branches of the trees, like sparks flying off a crackling campfire that light up a forest.

We watched this event until the moon rose overhead and the lightning bugs coupled, finding their private spaces out of our view. Everything felt alive. It was real life, in real time. As if a gossamer curtain was parted and we were allowed into an alternate universe, only briefly, until the veil closed again and all went dark and receded in the stillness. Everything seemed strangely unfamiliar—like we had been abducted, travelled to another planet, and put back down again in the same place, but in another time.

Reluctantly we came inside. My father asked for some hot tea. His voice was hushed as if we had just been in church and were still feeling reverent. My mother turned off the TV. There were no pundits or commentators or analysis needed. I thought to myself . . . *when my father passes from this world, he won't remember what global crisis stole the headlines that evening, but he will remember how the lightning bugs filled the entire galaxy on that night.*

ACKNOWLEDGEMENTS

COME CLOSER is the product of the force of nature seeking a voice. I thank the ancient ones and all the natural realm for the honor of being the vehicle for putting this voice into words. My sincerest appreciation for my muse who, parting the veil between worlds whispers to my soul.

COME CLOSER would not have given birth without the unwavering guidance and generous support of my editor and coach Raven Lamoreux-Dodd who acted as a midwife during the long process of bringing forth a new creation. Also, my dear friend LeeAnn Austin whose powerful insights were invaluable in keeping me encouraged.

My experiences at the Findhorn Foundation in Findhorn, Scotland and the introduction there to the fairy realm by Margot Brock and Lazaris were the validation of everything I knew intuitively as a child and the confirmation to proceed with transmitting the book.

I am deeply grateful to Blue Spruce Standing Deer and his wife Marti Fenton-White Deer Song for opening their cozy home in Taos, New Mexico, where for months I slept on the couch in the library to be around their wonderful energy and do ceremony to greet the sunrise. That experience was humbling and transformational and the inspiration for an entirely new story.

To all sentient beings everywhere . . .

Thank you! Thank you! Thank you!

CONTACT
INFORMATION

If you would like to contact me, please email me or visit my website. I would love to hear from you.

milda@mildavaivada.com
www.mildavaivada.com

MILDA VAIVADA

Enhance Magic · Embrace Mystery · Expect Miracles

Made in United States
North Haven, CT
19 October 2022

25634854R00054